I0424529

I remember

Sivadasan Channar

An
Alummood Publication

Other works by Sivadasan Channar

Slices of My Life   ...   2009

I remember

Sivadasan Channar

I remember

Copyright © 2010 by Sivadasan Madhavan Channar

All rights reserved.

No part of this book may be
reproduced in any manner without the
written permission of the author.

Cover
SASHA

ISBN: 1-45370-098-6
EAN: 139781453700983

Printed and published in the USA
by
Alummood Publications
www.Alummoottil.com

Distributed through
www.createspace.com/3469376

This book
Is dedicated to
The memory of Sasha
1995-2010

Sasha
December, 1995 – May, 2010

Author's Note

The loss of a pet who was also a most trusted friend is a traumatic event in anybody's life. It is as painful as losing a child. Unlike in the case of human beings, we take it for granted that terminating a pet's life for various reasons is acceptable. After all, it is an animal, and its life can never equal that of a human.

Thousands of pets are euthanized every day. The staff at most animal clinics go through this as part of their normal routines. However, when an individual is faced with the end of a beloved family pet, the normal rules fall by the wayside.

I had Sasha since she was eight weeks old. She was such a gentle and dignified dog that, in her fifteen and half years, she never made a single enemy. She loved everyone and everything. She loved children, and every child who came to the park near our house knew her, and loved her. On top of this, she was absolutely gorgeous. She was not much of a watchdog except for the normal respect people attributed to a German Sheppard.

When her body was ravaged by age, I had to rely on the advice of her veterinarian. I wanted her to have a dignified end. I could not allow her to die alone in the hands of others. Forewarned of my personal trauma, I summoned every bit of courage I could muster, and stayed with her through her end. I was not prepared for the casualness of pet euthanasia. It was just normal stuff for them. A few minutes of an animal's pain during its end stage, even when there were clearly better alternatives, was routine. An extra needle and the tranquilizer first were all it required to make her end the least painful and the most humane.

It affected me profoundly. I owed it to my dearest friend to be with her at her end. I am not convinced that euthanasia is better than natural death even if living is painful.

Sivadasan Channar

Herndon, VA.
May 15, 2010

I remember

I remember the first time we met.
You were such a small ball of fur.
Apprehensive at first, but hopeful that
You would catch my eye and heart.

I remember how sorry I was when
Someone else came and took you home
Still just six weeks old, I was happy that
You found a good home and a good master.

I remember how happy I was when
Several weeks later, you were abandoned.
Finally, I was reunited with you, two lost friends,
Perhaps, from many past lives together.

I remember how happy you were to be
With me, your dearest friend and master,
Where there is nothing like home,
Sweet home, your very own place.

I remember how you loved the woods,
The fields, the birds and the animals,
Most of all, the newborn calves
In the farmer's pasture behind.

I remember

I remember how often you came home
Sheepishly, after a roll in the cow manure,
To the inevitable scolding and the
Predictable hose down to follow.

I remember the day you met your mommy.
How terrified she was of a ten month old you,
As you ran up to greet her, your eyes
Sparkling with joy and love.

I remember how you loved Anand, my son.
How together you wandered and explored the woods.
How sad were you for days, when your friend
Went back to his school far, far away.

I remember you were only two, you were
Not a barker as I never heard you bark before,
Until that night when you discovered the little
Black baby snake in our living room.

I remember how you barked and barked.
It was two in the morning, and the poor snake
Was scared out of its wits, all curled up in a corner.
Under your supervision, we safely put it outside.

I remember how you hated to be left alone,
And how anxious were you for my return.
As if by sixth sense, you could tell the exact
Time my car will come down the driveway.

I remember how you ran around the house,
And around the yard, to express your joy
At the sight of me, at the end of the day,
To celebrate your victory at gaining me back.

I remember how I made you a long dog run,
Between the house and the old maple tree,
And how you enjoyed your freedom to run,
Instead of cooped up in a small pen.

I remember how you used to tear down the
Flower bushes to protest your confinement,
And how you brought home a dead rabbit
That you did not catch, to show us your hunting skill.

I remember how you knew all of my children,
Even when you met them for the first time,
The joy and your unconditional
Love and devotion to your family.

I remember how you welcomed my grandson,
As a newborn infant and instinctly taking
Charge of his protection, you knew
What he meant to you and me.

I remember how you knew that I belonged
To you and only you, evenings, weekends and
Holidays, and how you must be with me
Wherever I went, walking or riding.

I remember

I remember how gentle you were to the other dogs
Never once did you bark at any. You would sit and
Watch, and look at me asking whether you could
Go and meet even the most vicious ones.

I remember how you loved your friends Ollie and
Briscoe. You would gladly give Briscoe your bone,
And let Ollie eat your food and drink from your bowl,
Just happy they were your friends for life.

I remember how some were afraid of dogs, and
Were terrified at the sight of you for the first time,
Only to leave assured that some dogs were gentle,
And full of love in spite of their sizes, certainly you.

I remember at five, how gorgeous you were.
With a show dog stance, and a perfect body,
You were a looker, almost perfect, that made
Dog lovers turn around to take a second glance.

I remember how you loved to ride in the car.
Even on a hot day you would rather be out riding
Than comfortably be cool in the house,
With your nose against the wind, the only way to go.

I remember how young and bouncy you were once,
You could walk for miles and never get tired.
A short nap and you were ready to go
Until I could go no further.

I remember how you loved our morning and evening
Walks. The smells on the ground you could sniff
For ever, and the sights and the sounds that
Kept you dragging me around the block.

I remember how much you enjoyed watching
The children, waiting for the school bus in the morning.
How you would stop and wait for someone to
Say hello, and possibly a pat on your head.

I remember how happy you were to stop and
Play with the little children in the park,
How you made friends with the little
Girl who was afraid of strangers and animals.

I remember Halloween. The children would come
In the evening to collect candies, the small ones first.
How you would lie by the door to hand them their fares,
A 'hello Sasha' was all you expected in return.

I remember how sad you felt, and laid down
In protest, and never looked up, when on
Some hot summer days, mommy and I
Left you home when we went shopping.

I remember how fast you forgave us, and
Anxiously stood at the door with happiness
Watching every step we made, as we emptied the car,
And brought the groceries inside.

I remember

I remember how I wished you could
Only say what you believed, what a mighty
Hunter daddy must be to bring
Home all that chicken for you.

I remember how content you were to
Eat only chicken and rice, day after day,
As your poor stomach could stand no other
Dog food, not even the best as they claimed.

I remember how happily your mom cooked
All that fresh chicken for you in a pot.
A total vegan who never touched
Meat before you came into her life.

I remember what a sloppy eater you were
You used to splatter the food all around your dish.
By the time you were through, the place was a mess,
And how I grumbled as I cleaned after you.

I remember how frightened you were of
The summer rains and the lightning.
How you would curl up under my chair
When the firecrackers went up on the 4th of July.

I remember how you could sense when it rained
In Roanoke, and the wind was bringing the clouds east.
How nervous and anxious you used to get
Anticipating the inevitable lightning and thunder.

I remember how you loved to chase the squirrels
In our backyard, and how they used to scold you
And call you names in 'squirreleeze' from their
Safe perches half way up the tree.

I remember how you insisted to be with me
Every time I stepped out into the backyard,
How you loved to lay there in front of the barn
While inside I made toys for the children.

I remember how prickly your pain was
Of our separations, as we had to leave
You in the kennel for any of our overnight
Absences or any of our out of town travels.

I remember how you would make it perfectly
Clear to us that you did not appreciate being
'Abandoned' even for a short time, yet to forgot it
Soon in your enthusiasm for our reunion.

I remember how you enjoyed all the trips we took
To Stafford, our old house, and to Chester to see Will,
Ollie and Brisco. How you knew our destinations
As we exited the highway, miles before reaching there.

I remember how you loved my friend's lakeside house
To watch the geese and the ducks lazily floating
Over the water, under the clear fall sky,
The young ones close behind their parents

I remember

I remember how one day you got too close to the water,
The geese formed an army in Vee around the young.
With loud and angry trumpeting calls, how they
Swam towards you, and how hastily you retreated.

I remember how we changed our lifestyles for you,
We skipped all excursions where we could not take you.
At times, we took turns to stay home with you
While you kept your vigil at the door for the other.

I remember how you loved to come to the airport
To meet me as I returned home.
You were proud as you looked out the window
And greeted me with the warmth only you could give.

I remember how sensitive you were to my scolding.
For hours you laid in your bed with sad eyes,
Till I called you to my side and reassured you
What a good girl you were, and how you brightened up.

I remember how old age crept upon us.
It seemed all of a sudden our bones became brittle,
Our joints beyond repair, aching at every step,
Each step harder, to remind us of the youth gone by.

I remember how you stumbled and fell
On a splendid summer evening,
How you struggled in vain to push yourself up
With those feeble legs as they slipped away from you.

I remember how hurt I was when the Vet said
It was over, your days were numbered.
How angry I was, how matter of fact it was to them.
You were just a dog, except you were my best friend.

I remember how determined we were to struggle along
As long as we could, go a little further, a few more days.
Even with all the pain, life was infinitely better,
The fear of the unknown, the path with no way back.

I remember the day they asked me to bring you
To the clinic for the last time.
How we went for our last walk early in the morning,
One last walk, one last sniff of the familiar smells.

I remember how bravely you walked into the clinic.
How sure you were that your faith in me was total,
Though, I could sense that your sixth sense told you
That it was your last day, it was our farewell march.

I remember what they told me, it was painless.
You fall to sleep and slowly your heart would stop.
Painless? How unbearable it was to watch them
Try to push the large needle into your feeble veins.

I remember how I yelled at them to stop.
There had to be a better way than the torture.
Even if only for a few minutes, where was the painless?
It was my heart they were stabbing with the needle.

I remember

I remember demanding why not use a small syringe and
Sedate you first before the lethal stuff.
It was more expensive, it took more time they said.
You deserved better; you were my friend, not just a dog.

I remember how you looked at me with sad eyes
As the small needle went in and you cried softly.
You bravely leaned on my shoulder as I reassured you.
You slumped slowly as you fell asleep, head in my lap.

I remember letting them push the large catheter
Into your veins, your limp body offered no resistance.
I looked the other way as the vet pumped the poison
Into your vein, and into your heart.

I remember I could not stop stroking your head
The vet said it would take only thirty seconds.
Through my tears, I could feel your life slip away.
Moments later your heart finally stopped.

I remember looking at you, as you lay lifeless in my lap.
You were alive a moment ago, and now you were gone.
I wondered whether you could still see me weeping over
Your lifeless body, the one walked into the death trap.

I remember how humble I felt and how noble you were.
Your faultless faith over my senseless betrayal.
No matter how every one consoled me and justified it,
I knew in my heart that you were far above me.

I remember how I grieved, my inconsolable grief.
Everyone said time would heal the wound,
Time lessens the pain, time lessens the burden.
Yet, the guilt of my betrayal never goes away.

I remember of you when I take my solitary walks,
When I see a squirrel in the backyard,
When I see the little children in the park,
When I see people walking their dogs.

I remember the neighborhood Calico Cat came by.
He came to visit his old friend and to say hello.
He looked at me as if asking where his friend was,
He seemed to understand, and went away sad.

I remember of you when the school bus goes by,
When the children walk by our house early in the
morning, when they gather at the bus stop.
When I pass them by, they look at the lonely old man.

I remember of you when no one remembers me,
On father's day, on my birthday, even on Christmas day.
I remember how much you gave me for so little in return
While many care so little for so much I gave them.

I remember you my dear friend, my dear Sasha,
What you could teach the world about love and care.
A friend stands by you when everyone else is gone.
I remember you, I always will until the end of my day.

I remember

Sasha as a puppy

Sasha as a 1 year old

Sasha as a 2 year old

I remember

Sasha as a 2 year old

A young Sasha as 5 year old in a Rare moment

I remember

Sasha as an Old Lady at 14

www.ingramcontent.com/pod-product-compliance
Lightning Source LLC
Chambersburg PA
CBHW050355290526
45785CB00006B/2775